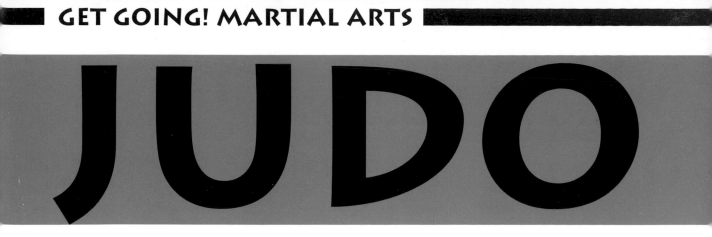

JUDO

NEIL MORRIS

D0100223

Heinemann
LIBRARY

H **www.heinemann.co.uk**
Visit our website to find out more information about **Heinemann Library** books.

To order:
☎ Phone 44 (0) 1865 888066
▤ Send a fax to 44 (0) 1865 314091
▭ Visit the Heinemann Bookshop at www.heinemann.co.uk/library to browse our catalogue and order online.

First published in Great Britain by Heinemann Library, Halley Court, Jordan Hill, Oxford OX2 8EJ, a division of Reed Educational and Professional Publishing Ltd. Heinemann is a registered trademark of Reed Educational & Professional Publishing Limited.

OXFORD MELBOURNE AUCKLAND JOHANNESBURG BLANTYRE
GABORONE IBADAN PORTSMOUTH NH (USA) CHICAGO

Designed by Ken Vail Graphic Design
Originated by Dot Gradations
Printed by Wing King Tong in Hong Kong.

ISBN 0 431 11040 9
05 04 03 02 01
10 9 8 7 6 5 4 3 2 1

500612272

British Library Cataloguing in Publication Data

Morris, Neil, 1946–
  Judo. – (Get Going! Martial arts)
  1. Judo – Juvenile literature
  I. Title
  796.8'152

Acknowledgements
The Publishers would like to thank the following for permission to reproduce photographs:
Action Images/Tim Matthews, p.8.; Bob Willingham, pp. 5, 6, 7, 21, 27, 28. All other photographs by Trevor Clifford.

Cover photograph reproduced with permission of Empics.

Our thanks to Sandra Beale, Director of Coaching, National Association of Karate and Martial Art Schools for her comments in the preparation of this book. Our thanks also to Mick Ellis and the students of Harlow Judo Club.

Every effort has been made to contact copyright holders of any material reproduced in this book. Any omissions will be rectified in subsequent printings if notice is given to the Publisher.

Words appearing in the text in bold, **like this**, are explained in the Glossary.

CONTENTS

! Do remember that martial arts need to be taught by a qualified, registered instructor, or teacher. Don't try any of the techniques and movements in this book without such an instructor present.

WHAT IS JUDO?

Judo is a Japanese martial art in which students, called *judokas*, use **grappling** and throwing **techniques**. The word judo means 'gentle way'. This is a good way to describe it because much of its skill lies in using balanced techniques to overcome an opponent. Like other martial arts, judo offers the chance to practise demanding physical routines and learn about self-defence, as well as take part in a competitive sport.

People who know little about judo may think of it as a rough, or even violent sport. But in judo no one ever tries to hurt an opponent. It is the 'gentle way' because many techniques depend on the judoka apparently giving in to an opponent's attack until it is just the right moment to strike back.

The founder of judo, Jigoro Kano (see pages 6–7), believed that judo allowed a smaller, lighter, weaker person to overcome a larger, heavier, more powerful opponent. For example, if the stronger judoka tries to push his opponent, the less powerful judoka can move back unexpectedly and not lose his balance. Then the person pushing leans forward, goes off balance and can easily be thrown down.

Young judokas get to grips with each other.

MENTAL DISCIPLINE

Judo is a form of exercise that uses the mind as well as the body. Its founder believed that judokas could train themselves to achieve 'maximum efficiency with minimum effort' by co-ordinating mind and body in attack and defence. The example on page 4 is a good illustration. A judoka must always be alert, controlled and calm, ready to react to any situation. Both competitors should get something out of judo, rather than simply being a winner or a loser.

WHERE TO LEARN AND PRACTISE

This book gives you lots of ideas about how to set about starting judo. It also shows and explains some judo techniques, so that you can understand and practise them. But always remember that you cannot learn a martial art just from a book. Any serious student of judo must go to regular lessons with a qualified teacher, so that all the techniques are learned properly and then repeated many times.

YOUR JUDO CLUB

Choose your club carefully. It should have an experienced teacher and belong to a judo association. The list on page 31 shows where you can get information about clubs.

Members of a modern judo club.

JUDO – THE BEGINNINGS

Judo developed from an ancient Japanese form of unarmed combat, physical training and self-defence called *jujitsu*, which means 'gentle skill'. Jujitsu was practised centuries ago by *samurai*, Japanese warriors, who learned its skills along with archery, swordsmanship and spear fighting. Monks, merchants and travellers were also trained in jujitsu. Original jujitsu included **techniques** such as kicking and choking, which were used to fight off and disable an opponent.

In 1882, a young Japanese man named Jigoro Kano turned jujitsu into a modern martial art which he called judo. When Kano was eleven, his family moved from the country to Tokyo, which had just been made the **imperial** capital of Japan. Kano was small for his age, and at first he was bullied at his new school. He decided to learn jujitsu as a means of self-defence. His new-found confidence and physical skills meant that he was never picked on again.

Jigoro Kano (1860–1938), founder of judo.

After continuing to train in jujitsu while studying at Tokyo University, Kano decided to take its best features and turn them into a means of personal development. He removed the dangerous kicks and punches, introduced regular practice in falling **techniques**, and drew up a set of rules for all judo students. He named his new school *Kodokan*, 'the place for studying the way'. The name is still used for the world headquarters of judo in Tokyo, Japan. When the chief of Tokyo's police organized a contest between Kodokan students and traditional jujitsu schools, Kano's judo pupils won.

Kodokan International Judo Centre, Tokyo, has more than a million visitors a year. It also houses a judo hall of fame.

By 1887, the Kodokan school had more than 1,500 pupils. Judo's popularity quickly grew throughout Japan, where it was soon taught in schools. In 1889, Jigoro Kano travelled to Europe to spread his **philosophy**. The first judo club in Europe was founded in London in 1918. Judo quickly spread worldwide, and interest was increased at the same time in the United States by the enthusiasm shown by President Theodore Roosevelt. Kano also believed that judo was good for women. He opened special training halls for them, despite severe criticism at the time.

After Jigoro Kano's death, his martial art grew very quickly as a major competitive sport. Judo also became an Olympic sport in 1964 (see pages 28–29).

EQUIPMENT

Judo is performed in a special outfit called a *judogi*, or *gi* (sounds like *gee*) for short. It is best to buy a gi through your club. The judogi is usually all white, but in some high-level competitions one of the two competitors wears a blue judogi.

The judogi is made up of a pair of trousers and a loose jacket tied at the waist with a belt. Girls wear a white T-shirt under the jacket. Gis are usually sold with a white belt, which is the right colour for a beginner. You will see that the gi has stronger material across the shoulders, around the collar and at the knees, so that it is not easily torn.

The blue judogi is worn only for high-level competitions.

Always keep your gi clean and neat, and wash it after each training session. A neat and tidy appearance shows that you have the right attitude to training. Inside the training hall, called a *dojo*, you must always have bare feet. Japanese-style slippers called *zori*, or flip-flops, are useful to keep your feet clean as you walk from the changing room to the dojo.

PUTTING ON THE GI

1 Put the trousers on first. Pull the drawstring and tie it with a bow. Next put on the jacket, crossing the left side over the right side.

2 To tie the belt, pull it across your stomach first, keeping the two ends equal.

3 Cross the ends over at the back and bring them back to the front.

4 Cross the left end over the right, then pull it up behind both layers of the belt.

5 Tie the free ends together right over left and pull them through to finish the knot.

⚠ SAFETY

In order not to harm yourself or anyone else, don't wear a watch or any jewellery. Keep your fingernails and toenails trimmed short. Tie long hair back, but never with metal clips.

Make sure that you are fit enough to be very active, and don't train if you are ill. Exercise should not hurt, so never push yourself to the point where you feel pain. Tell your instructor if you suffer from any medical condition.

All martial arts can be dangerous if they are not performed properly. Never fool around inside or outside the training hall – or at home or in school – by showing off or pretending to have a real fight.

IN THE DOJO

TRADITIONAL COURTESY

It is important for any judoka to show respect to everyone and everything to do with judo. Polite behaviour and discipline are of great importance in all martial arts. Judo students must show respect and **courtesy** to opponents, other students and to the art of judo itself. Everyone must learn the rules and courtesies of judo, and in the dojo the word of the *sensei* (judo instructor) is law.

To begin a session, students make a kneeling bow to their sensei. To do this, first kneel down on the floor. Point your toes and sit back on your calves, keeping your back straight and looking forwards. Then bend forwards, sliding your hands down your thighs and on to the mat just in front of your knees. Let your eyes follow the bow to the floor, but do not let your face go too close to the mat.

The kneeling bow shows great respect.

Before and after every practice, and each time they change partners within a practice session, judokas make a standing bow to one another. All judokas, from beginners to Olympic finalists, make this bow at the beginning of contests.

To make the bow, stand in a relaxed way, looking straight ahead. Your feet should be about a shoulder-width apart and your hands should be relaxed at your sides. Then bow smoothly by bending your upper body forwards, but not too far. Let your eyes follow the bow to the floor, and slide your hands forwards so that the palms cover your knees. Hold the position for a second, then straighten up again.

When you are bowing to a partner, make sure that there is enough space between you so that you don't bump heads. One and a half arms' distance is about right.

This is a standing bow by two partners.

KATA CONTESTS

Kata (which means 'form') is a demonstration of pre-arranged judo **techniques**, performed by a judoka with a co-operating partner. The techniques are linked together by a common theme. One of the themes is based on 21 techniques originally used by ancient warriors. There are kata contests and championships, and kata is also used at grading exams.

WARMING UP

Judo gives you a lot of hard, physical exercise. It is important to warm your body up and stretch your muscles before training, so that you will not injure yourself. At your club you will always start a session with some warm-up exercises. You might begin by walking or jogging on the spot for a couple of minutes, before doing some stretching exercises.

! IMPORTANT

- Never exercise too hard when it is very hot or humid. Normally, the cool, dry dojo will ensure that this is not the case.

- Never exercise or practise judo when you are ill or injured.

- Try not to breathe too hard and fast when you are exercising or resting.

- Don't hold your breath while you are exercising or practising judo.

- When you are stretching, you should always remain comfortable and your muscles should not hurt. If you feel pain, stop at once.

- Don't stand still immediately after you have been exercising. You should begin your judo exercises immediately after warming up.

WINDMILLS

Turn your arms like the sails of a windmill.

1 Stand up straight with your arms by your sides.

2 Swing your right arm forwards, up and round behind you in a circle. Keep your arm straight and reach high at the top of the circle. Repeat five times.

3 Do the same exercise with the left arm.

4 Then repeat the exercise with both arms at the same time.

CALF STRETCH

The calf muscle is at the back of your lower leg.

1 Stand up straight and put one foot about 30 centimetres ahead of the other.

2 Raise the toes of your forward foot as far as you can, keeping your heel firmly on the floor. Hold this position for a count of ten.

3 Repeat the stretch with the other leg.

SHOULDER ROLLS

1 Stand up straight with your hands by your sides.

2 Roll your shoulders in a backward direction, making as big a circle as you can. Do ten rolls.

3 Repeat the exercise, rolling your shoulders forward this time.

BREAKFALLS

Many people are afraid of falling and being thrown when they are new to judo. This makes them stiffen up so that it is more likely that they will be hurt. So the first thing to learn in judo is how to break, or soften, a fall. You do this by rolling, tumbling and using the arms to absorb the shock. Breakfall **techniques** take the force out of the impact. This in turn builds up your confidence and takes the fear out of being thrown.

PRACTISING BREAKFALLS

It is best to practise breakfalls on your own at first, and two easy techniques are shown here. Always use a judo mat. Most beginners find it easier to fall either to their right or left side. In competitions you will be thrown to either side, so it is really important to practise your breakfalls on both sides.

As your confidence grows, you can practise breakfalls with a partner. At first it is very important that the thrower guides his or her partner onto the mat, trying to help the partner learn rather than hurting him or her.

JUDO MATS

As soon as you start falling, you will realize how important the judo mat, or *tatami*, is. Tatamis are no longer made of traditional Japanese rice-straw matting, but they are specially made to take some of the force out of falls. At first, a special crash-mat may also be used. You don't want to hurt yourself, so always practise on the judo mat, and do not be tempted to try practising anywhere else.

BACK BREAKFALL

1 Stand with your arms straight out in front of you.

2 Bend your knees and go into a squatting position as you let yourself fall backwards. Tuck your chin in and curve your back as you start to fall.

3 Slap down hard with the palms of both hands, keeping your head up and off the mat. The harder you slap, the easier the landing.

SIDE BREAKFALL

1 Squat down on the mat and look straight ahead. Put your right arm out and thrust your right leg forwards and diagonally across your body.

2 Roll to the right, and as your bottom touches the mat, strike the mat with your right arm. Keep your chin tucked in and your head off the mat.

THROWING

Throwing **techniques** form the basis of judo. Most of the throws rely more on skill and timing than on strength. The judoka performing the throw usually tries to move their partner into an unbalanced position, which makes the throw much easier. Groups of throws are named according to which part of the body the thrower uses to gain power. There are hip techniques, hand techniques, and foot and leg techniques. Beginners go through the moves slowly, learning them step by step, and then putting all the steps together in one smooth action.

NAMES OF THROWS AND THROWER

Groups of throws and individual techniques all have a Japanese and an English name. These may seem difficult at first, but you soon pick them up. Hip techniques are called *koshi-waza* and hand techniques *te-waza*.

In judo, Japanese terms are used for the two partners or opponents. The judoka performing a move such as a throw is called *tori*. The partner, who is on the receiving end of the move, is called *uke*.

MAJOR HIP THROW

This throw, called *o-goshi* in Japanese, is one of the most commonly used first throws for beginners. It is one of the hip techniques, in which the thrower uses a powerful hip action to lift the opponent up and over.

1 Step across in front of uke with your right foot as you grip uke's sleeve with your left hand.

2 Drive your right hand around uke's back, bend your knees, and pull uke's hip against your back.

3 Straighten your legs, bend forwards and pull uke over your hips and back. Keep hold of uke's sleeve with your right hand and help break the fall.

BODY DROP

The body drop, or *tai-otoshi*, is one of the hand techniques, so called because tori uses his hands to get uke moving and unbalance him. Hand techniques are especially useful for small judokas and have a high scoring rate in competition.

First push your opponent backwards. When he pushes back, use the force of his push to pull him forwards. Then turn to the left, placing your right calf across uke's right ankle, and throw him across your leg.

FOOT AND LEG TECHNIQUES

Most foot and leg **techniques** involve throwing the opponent by moving one of his or her legs away. This may be by using a sweeping, hooking or tripping action, especially when the opponent is least expecting it or is off-balance. Timing is very important. As with all the other techniques in this book, please don't try to do this outside the dojo, as it could be very dangerous.

FOULS

Remember that you are never allowed to kick in judo, so you must learn the foot and leg techniques correctly. The techniques are all part of the overall group of throws and involve grasping the opponent, not just kicking out or tripping at random. Attempting to throw an opponent by entwining a leg around his or her leg is also a foul.

FOOT SWEEP

In the advancing foot sweep, or *deashi-barai*, you force your opponent to take a step forwards and then sweep uke's foot away.

1 Push forwards against your partner, and then step backwards to make him follow you.

2 As uke steps forwards onto his left foot, sweep it away with the sole of your right foot, just as he is about to put it on the mat and put his weight on it. At the same time pull down and out on uke's sleeve with your right hand.

3 If your timing is right, your opponent will go down as if he has slipped on a banana skin. Remember to make a big, bold sweeping action from the hip, not just a little tap with the foot.

FOOT REAP

In the major inner reap, or *o-uchi-gari*, the attacker drives forward off the back foot and uses the other leg to reap, which means to cut or clip, one of the opponent's legs to throw him backwards.

The major inner reap is a kind of foot reap.

LEG THROW

The inner thigh throw, or *uchi-mata*, is one of the most successful and popular moves in judo. Tori turns towards uke, steps between his legs, and sweeps upwards with his forward leg against uke's inside thigh. Uke is thrown over the forward leg and lands on his back.

The inner thigh throw is a kind of leg throw.

GROUNDWORK

In competitive judo, a player tries to put his or her opponent in such a position that he or she has to **submit**, or give up. This is the aim of many judo throws. Moves on the mat are called groundwork, and usually involve **grappling** for position and holding the opponent down.

For beginners and juniors, groundwork is made up of **hold-downs**. These involve pinning the opponent down and holding that position for up to 25 seconds. Obviously the opponent will try to wriggle free, and you might think that they will be able to if they are heavier or stronger. But just like all other aspects of judo, skilful **techniques** can be used to overcome sheer strength, especially using body positions correctly.

SCARF HOLD

This head-and-shoulder pin is one of the first hold-downs to learn. It is called *kesa-gatame* in Japanese, and is named after the traditional scarf, or diagonal sash, that was worn in ancient Japan. In fact, Japanese archers still wear the *kesa*. The name comes from the diagonal hold you put on your opponent.

1 Your opponent has fallen at your side. Very quickly drop down and sit in the space between his right arm and his body, holding his shoulders with both hands. Wedge your hip tightly against your opponent's body as you put your right arm around his neck.

2 Grip your opponent's jacket tightly with both hands, and spread your legs wide to keep you stable. Lower your head, and hold your opponent in that position.

LEARNING ABOUT ARMLOCKS AND STRANGLEHOLDS

There are two more techniques that only seniors use. These are armlocks and strangleholds. They can obviously be very dangerous, so there are many rules about how they can be used. Juniors are not allowed to use them, so don't try any of the armlocks or strangleholds that you may see seniors using.

Kate Howey of Great Britain, in the blue gi, used an armlock to win a bout at the 2000 Olympic Games in Sydney.

SUBMISSION

To stop a hold-down, the defender taps on the mat or the attacker's body twice. When this happens, or if the defender shows in any other way that they want you to stop, you must release the pressure immediately in order to avoid injury.

SACRIFICE THROWS AND COMBINATIONS

Sacrifice throws are when the judoka appears to sacrifice, or give up, a good position. In fact the judoka uses them as a way to gain a different, unexpected advantage. Sacrifice throws usually involve judokas going down on the mat on their back or side and throwing the opponent with their legs.

Sacrifice throws are spectacular. Though they are good for beginners to practise, remember that in a competition sacrifices can leave you open to attack if they are not done well.

STOMACH THROW

Tomoe-nage, sometimes called the whirl or crescent throw, often scores high in competitions. It is useful when your opponent has tried a move such as a foot reap but has failed.

1 Drop down onto your back as you hold on to your opponent's jacket. As you pull uke towards you, raise your leg and put your foot in his or her stomach.

2 Straighten your leg sharply and hang on to uke's jacket so that he or she whirls over you onto his or her back.

Obviously, timing is very important in this move so that you don't hurt yourself or your opponent. You must remember also that it is a risky move, because if you fail to throw your opponent, he or she could easily drop down and put you in a **hold-down** such as the scarf hold (see pages 20–21).

COMBINATION THROWING TECHNIQUES

You can also practise putting two or more throws together, which will be useful when you come to compete later. Some of the possible double moves are called linked **techniques** (*renzoku-waza*) when they are in the same direction. Others are called combination techniques (*renraku-waza*) when the first technique in one direction breaks the opponent's balance, and the second technique follows in the other direction.

Some of the throws already described can be made into combinations. A good example would be to try the body drop (see page 17), and then if this does not work, switch straight into a major inner reap in the other direction (page 19).

Combining body drop and major inner reap. Step 1, attempted body drop.

Combining body drop and major inner reap. Step 2, major inner reap.

DEFENCE BECOMES ATTACK

In all competitive sports, players must learn to defend as well as attack. In judo, however, defence is always seen as an opportunity to **counter-attack**. Competition rules state that it is an offence to take up too defensive an attitude, either by backing away or by not attacking. This rule and the whole attitude of attack make judo much more fun to learn, practise and watch.

COUNTER-ATTACK

For every judo move there is a counter-move. Some moves are more difficult to counter than others, and you will learn this with experience. You will also learn that it is much easier to counter a badly timed or incorrectly performed move by your opponent. All the same, you have to time your counter-attack perfectly, too.

You can counter-attack just as your opponent shifts his or her balance to attack you. Or you can wait until the attack is under way. For example, you could ride or block an inner thigh throw (see page 19) and counter with a body drop (page 17). Or the other way round. There are lots of counter-moves in groundwork, too.

Here is a very simple, but effective counter-attack.

1 Your opponent tries a foot sweep. You see it coming and quickly lift your foot.

2 The opponent's foot passes under yours.

3 You then help the opponent's foot on its way, in the same direction, forcing him or her off-balance.

FREE PRACTICE

The best way to get used to defending and counter-attacking is during free practice (or *randori*), when you compete against an opponent. It is called 'free' because it is not pre-planned and does not involve **drill**. The idea of randori is that it gives players the opportunity to practise their skills in a competitive situation. There is no referee, so it is up to the two partners to help each other practise and enjoy themselves.

Sometimes clubs also organize a session of practice competitions with rules and points strictly enforced. This gives more advanced judokas the experience of serious competition.

A free practice session in the dojo.

! COOLING DOWN

It is important to cool down gently after vigorous exercise such as judo. You can do this by jogging or walking, and by deep breathing and gently stretching as you did when you warmed up (see pages 12–13). Some judokas like to cool down by doing some kata to music.

GRADING

When you join a judo club, you should get a licence and membership of your national judo association. By regularly paying a small amount of money, you will also be covered by insurance. This means you will be entitled to a larger amount of money if you are injured while practising judo through your club.

Your licence book also gives you the right to be properly graded, and to attend regional and national competitions, when you are ready. As you make your way from beginner to expert, your level of skill is shown by different coloured belts.

BELT RANKS

Grades and belt colours vary in different countries, but the following is a common system. Juniors are normally divided into three age groups – 8 to 9, 10 to 12 and 13 to 15. Juniors have a series of 18 grades called *mon*, each with its own distinctive belt.

Junior Grades			
Mon (grade)	Belt colour	Mon (grade)	Belt colour
1st	white, one red bar	10th	green, one red bar
2nd	white, two red bars	11th	green, two red bars
3rd	white, three red bars	12th	green, three red bars
4th	yellow, one red bar	13th	blue, one red bar
5th	yellow, two red bars	14th	blue, two red bars
6th	yellow, three red bars	15th	blue, three red bars
7th	orange, one red bar	16th	brown, one red bar
8th	orange, two red bars	17th	brown, two red bars
9th	orange, three red bars	18th	brown, three red bars

Seniors are aged 16 and over. They have their own series of 9 grades called *kyu*. Beginners wear a white belt.

Senior Grades			
Kyu (grade)	*Belt colour*	*Kyu (grade)*	*Belt colour*
9th	yellow	4th	blue
8th	orange	3rd	blue
7th	orange	2nd	brown
6th	green	1st	brown
5th	green		black

Black is the top belt, and the ultimate aim of every judoka. The black belt is split up into ten different degrees, or *dan*. Very few people in the history of judo have reached the top, 10th dan.

GRADING EXAMS

To move up a grade and gain a new belt, you take a grading exam. This is usually in two parts, covering practice and theory. There is a competition section, as well as a set of questions about judo to answer.

A grading exam in progress.

Grades are important and must be respected. You will notice, however, that expert judokas show total respect for lower grades and beginners. This is an important aspect of all the martial arts, and you should not worry too much about which belt colour you wear. Do your best to progress at your own pace, whatever age you are when you begin.

A WORLD SPORT

Judo became a serious competitive sport in 1930 when the first All-Japan Championships were held in Tokyo. After judo grew in popularity around the world, the International Judo Federation was founded in 1951. The first World Championships were held five years later.

Judo first became an Olympic sport for male competitors in 1964, at the Tokyo Games. The first Olympic gold medal was won by Japan, when Takehide Nakatani won the lightweight class. However, 15,000 Japanese home supporters were shocked when a Dutchman, Anton Geesink, beat the Japanese favourite for the open category. Now both men and women compete in the Olympic Games.

CONTEST RULES

Judo sporting contests take place on a 8-metre square mat, with extra danger and safety areas around it. Each bout is controlled by a referee in the contest area, and two judges, who remain at opposite corners outside the danger area. A men's bout lasts five minutes, a women's bout four minutes, and junior bouts last between two and four minutes. A timekeeper times the bout and the length of holds.

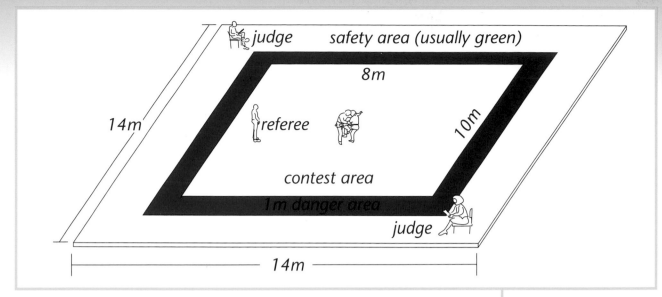

The two contestants wear red and white belts, so that the officials and spectators can tell them apart. It is now becoming quite usual for one of them to wear a blue judogi and the other a white one. To win the contest, a player has to score an *ippon*, or two *wazaris* (or *waza-aris*). If neither player achieves this, points are added up according to the number of wazaris, *yukos* and *kokas* scored (see below). One wazari beats any number of yukos, and one yuko beats any number of kokas. If the contest is a draw, the referee and judges decide on the winner.

This diagram shows the contest area for an international competition.

Score	Technique
ippon	skilful throw resulting in opponent landing with force on back; **submission** from armlock or stranglehold; 25-second **hold-down**
wazari	throw in which opponent lands partially on side; 21- to 25-second hold-down
yuko	throw which lacks force and opponent lands on side; 15- to 20-second hold-down
koka	throw from which opponent lands on thigh or buttocks; 10- to 15-second hold-down

Penalty points are deducted from players' scores for breaking the rules.

JAPANESE WORDS

The Japanese words are pronounced as written here. When you see the letters 'ai', say them like the English word 'eye'.

Japanese word	Meaning	Japanese word	Meaning
deashi-barai	advancing foot reap	*sensei*	judo instructor, teacher
dojo	training hall		
ippon	one full point	*tai-otoshi*	body drop
jujitsu	a martial art, means 'gentle skill'	*tatami*	mat
		te-waza	hand technique
kata	pattern, form	*tomoe-nage*	stomach, whirl or crescent throw
kesa-gatame	scarf hold		
Kodokan	a judo school, means 'the place for studying the way'	*tori*	in a pair of judo students, the one performing a move
koka	lowest judo score, means 'valuable'	*uchi-mata*	inner thigh throw
		uke	in a pair of judo students, the one on the receiving end of a move
koshi-waza	hip technique		
kyu	grade		
mon	junior grade		
o-goshi	major hip throw	*waza-ari* or *wazari*	a half point
o-uchi-gari	major inner reap		
randori	free practice	*yuko*	the third highest judo score, means 'valid'
renraku-waza	combination technique		
renzoku-waza	linked technique	*zori*	slippers

GLOSSARY

Counter-attack	to reply to an attack by an opponent with your own attack
courtesy	polite, considerate behaviour
drill	repeating something so you learn it well
grapple	to grip and wrestle with an opponent
hold-down	a move in which a judo student holds his opponent down on the ground
imperial	to do with an empire; the imperial capital was the capital of the Japanese Empire
philosophy	a set of beliefs
submit	to give up, especially when you are held down and cannot move (noun: submission)
technique	the way to perform a particular skill

BOOKS

First Action Skills: Judo by N. Adams, HarperCollins, London, 1992

Go for Sport: Judo by Tony Reay, Wayland, Hove, 1993

Judo for Juniors by Nicholas Soames, Stanley Paul, London, 1991

Junior Judo by Mike Leigh, Foulsham, Slough, 1996

Know the Game: Judo by Geoff Gleeson, A & C Black, London, 1995

Skilful Judo by Brian Caffary, A & C Black, London, 1992

Sports Skills: Judo by Norman Barrett, Wayland, Hove, 1993

The Young Martial Arts Enthusiast by David Mitchell, Dorling Kindersley, London, 1997

Top Sport: Martial Arts by Bernie Blackall, Heinemann Library, Oxford, 1998

USEFUL ADDRESSES

UK Sport
40 Bernard Street
London WC1N 1ST
020 7841 9500
www.uksport.gov.uk

Sport England
16 Upper Woburn Place
London WC1H 0QP
020 7273 1500
www.english.sports.gov.uk

Sport Scotland
Caledonia House
South Gyle
Edinburgh EH12 9DQ
0131 317 7200
www.sportscotland.org.uk

Sports Council for Wales
Sophia Gardens
Cardiff CF1 9SW
029 2030 0500
www.sports-council-wales.co.uk

Sports Council for
  Northern Ireland
Upper Malone Road
Belfast BT9 5LA
028 9038 1222
www.sportni.org

National Association of
  Karate & Martial Art
  Schools
Rosecraig
Bullockstone Road
Herne Bay CT6 7NL
01227 370055
www.nakmas.org.uk

Martial Arts
  Development
  Commission
PO Box 381
Erith DA8 1TF
01322 431440
www.madec.org

British Judo Association
7A Rutland Street
Leicester LE1 1RB
0116 255 9669
www.britishjudo.org.uk

International Judo
  Federation
21st Floor
Doosan Building
101–1 Ulchiro 1ka
Choong Ku
Seoul, South Korea
00 82 2 754 1075
www.ijf.org

Kodokan Judo Institute
16-30 Kasuga 1-chome
Bunkyo-ku
Tokyo 112, Japan
00 81 3818 4199
www.kadokan.org

Judo Federation of
  Australia
PO Box 919
Glebe
NSW 2037
02 9552 2770
www.ausport.gov.au/judo

INDEX

Titles in the *Get Going! Martial Arts* series include:

GET GOING! MARTIAL ARTS

JUDO

NEIL MORRIS

Hardback   0 431 11040 9

GET GOING! MARTIAL ARTS

KARATE

NEIL MORRIS

Hardback   0 431 11042 5

GET GOING! MARTIAL ARTS

KUNG FU

NEIL MORRIS

Hardback   0 431 11043 3

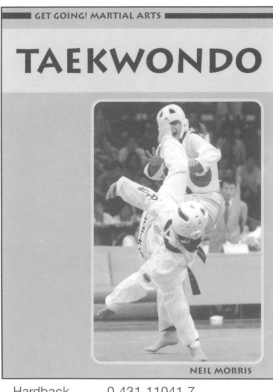

GET GOING! MARTIAL ARTS

TAEKWONDO

NEIL MORRIS

Hardback   0 431 11041 7

Find out about the other titles in this series on our website www.heinemann.co.uk/library